Ulwembu

EMPATHEATRE AND
THE BIG BROTHERHOOD

with the Urban Futures Centre

CREATED BY

Mpume Mthombeni

Neil Coppen

Dylan McGarry

Vumani Khumalo

Phumlani Ngubane

Ngcebo Cele

Sandile Nxumalo

Zenzo Msomi

WITS UNIVERSITY PRESS

Published in South Africa by:
Wits University Press
1 Jan Smuts Avenue
Johannesburg 2001

www.witspress.co.za

Copyright © Mpume Mthombeni, Neil Coppen and Dylan McGarry
Published edition © Wits University Press 2018
Images © Val Adamson

First published 2018

http://dx.doi.org.10.18772/32018061951

978-1-77614-195-1 (Print)
978-1-77614-196-8 (Web PDF)

Application to perform this work in public and to obtain a copy of the play
should be made to: Dramatic, Artistic and Literary Rights Organisation
(DALRO), P O Box 31627, Braamfontein, 2017. No performance may be
given unless a license has been obtained.

Copyeditor: Pat Tucker
Proofreader: Mirie van Rooyen
Cover design: Fire and Lion
Typesetter: Fire and Lion
Typeset in 10 point Minion Pro

Directed with a muscularity and sense of conviction, this beautifully researched and deeply felt performance takes advocacy theatre which talks to the man on the street to a level that is considerably deeper and theatrically more developed than convention dictates. Normally, you might hear the words 'community theatre' or 'advocacy drama' and shrink away from the product's aesthetic value, understanding it to be a mere one-dimensional extrapolation of bald ideologies. But the adjective 'mere' doesn't fit in any understanding of this poignant and hard hitting play.

Robyn Sassen, *My View*

Not only does *Ulwembu* present a compelling theatre experience, but its true-to-life format means that this team is taking the bull by the horns and using the Arts to take to the frontlines of the war against drugs.

Independent Online

… this production is not a stereotyped 'say no to drugs' play. It is a deeply-researched theatre project which is authentic, insightful, razor-sharp and frighteningly real. In fact, I would go as far as to say that this is educational theatre at its zenith.

ArtSmart Review

Ulwembu powerfully reveals the root causes of substance abuse.

South African Police Service

If you are brave enough to hear what is seldom heard on a issue that touches rich and poor - then you need to let your heart be touched by this talented team.

Father Tully, *Emmanuel Cathedral*

This play challenges us, in a very graphic way, to face up to the human face of the problem and recognise that we do not know who it will hurt and how.

Raymond Perrier, *Denis Hurley Centre*

Dedicated to Emmanuel Sithole

Contents

Acknowledgements ix

Foreword by Monique Marks xi

Introduction by Dylan McGarry xvii

Glossary and translation xxxi

Images from production xxxv

Ulwembu: the play script 1

Prologue: Our story 3

Scene 1: Behind the police station 4

Scene 2: The police station, captain's office 9

Scene 3: The school yard 10

Scene 4: Portia's house 13

Scene 5: Behind Emmanuel's sphaza shop 16

Scene 6: Behind Emmanuel's sphaza shop 17

Scene 7: The police station 19

Scene 8: Emmanuel's sphaza shop 21

Scene 9: Outside Emmanuel's sphaza shop 23

Scene 10: Outside Emmanuel's sphaza shop 25

Scene 11: Portia's house   31

Scene 12: Bongani's house   33

Scene 13: Outside Emmanuel's sphaza shop   36

Scene 14: Outside Emmanuel's sphaza shop   37

Scene 15: Bongani's house   40

Scene 16: Outside Emmanuel's sphaza shop   43

Scene 17: Sipho's room   44

Scene 18: Emmanuel's sphaza shop   45

Scene 19: Captain's office   46

Scene 20: Behind the police station   47

Scene 21: Bongani's house   49

Scene 22: Portia's house   52

Scene 23: Captain's office   57

Scene 24: Emmanuel's sphaza shop   58

Scene 25: On the street   60

Epilogue: Our story   61

Notes   62

The Authors   65

Acknowledgements

The project was led by writer/director Neil Coppen, actress/story-teller Mpume Mthombeni, Dylan McGarry (educational sociologist and artist) and the Big Brotherhood (Vumani Khumalo, Phumlani Ngubane, Ngcebo Cele, Sandile Nxumalo and Zenzo Msomi) in association with the Urban Futures Centre, Twist Theatre Development Project (Twist Durban), Think Theatre and the generous constant support of the Denis Hurley Centre.

The primary funders were the Open Society Foundation, Twist (www.twistprojects.co.za), the Urban Futures Centre, The Playhouse Company, the Denis Hurley Centre and the National Institute for Humanities and Social Science.

The project would not have been possible without the support of Monique Marks, Kira Ewrin, Emma Durden, Tina La Roux, Bryan Hiles, Margie Coppen, Kathryn Bennett, Rogers Ganesan, Stephanie Jenkins, Tamar Meskin, Raymond Perrier, Illa Thompson, Bongi Ngobese, Father Stephen Tully, Col. Vuyana, Pruthvi Karpoormath, Fathima Bi Bi Ally, Elena Naumkina, Cpt. Dingaan, Rob Chetty, Chris Overall, Commissioner Steve Middleton, Lloyd Gede, Greg Lomas, Carla-Dee Sims, Lynette Machado at Sad Sacks, Colwyn Thomas, Beata Bognar, Kathryn Bennett, Shaun Shelley, Val Adamson, Braam du Toit, Karen Logon, Iain (Ewok) Robinson, Don Fletcher, UKZN, DUT, Carrots & Peas at Kenneth Gardens, South African Police Services, Durban Metro Police, KZN Department of Health, *City Press*, Hillbrow Theatre and Gerard Bester.

Acknowledgements

Foreword

MAKING SENSE OF DRUG USE:
THE POWER OF *ULWEMBU*

I have never been directly involved in the creative arts. I have, throughout my life, lacked the confidence to view myself as a creative person, although I have come to realise that every person has the capacity to be creative. Not all of us, however, have the skills, talent and knowledge to be able to pull together a powerful production that rivets audiences and assists in making sense of very complex problems.

My personal inadequacies in regard to the creative arts were, in some ways, reinforced, as I became part of, then watched in absolute awe, the production of *Ulwembu* by the Big Brotherhood community theatre group. This highly skilled group of actors, directed by Neil Coppen and Dylan McGarry, brought to a number of stages (formal and informal) in both KwaZulu-Natal and Gauteng, a theatre production that will not be forgotten by any person who watched it.

Ulwembu, which focuses on the various spiderwebs tangled in the world of street-level drug use, is without doubt, a powerful and deeply researched presentation on the pathways into and out of problematic drug use. The play is situated in Durban, where smoking brown heroin mixed with a number of other (often toxic) compounds has become alarmingly widespread. Whoonga – the street name given to this heroin-based compound – is ubiquitous in Durban and in other parts of the country.

Immediately after using whoonga there is a sense of sedation and hypnotic calm, the withdrawal symptoms related to stopping (or attempting to stop) using are nothing short of horrendous. Nightmares, tremors, sweats, intense head and stomach pain, as well as heightened anxiety, all accompany withdrawal and act as a strong deterrent from abstaining or even reducing use. This horror is brilliantly portrayed in the play, providing the viewer and the reader with critical information about why 'just stopping' is an option that is unlikely to work.

But *Ulwembu* teaches us far more about street-level drug use. Arising out of Big Brotherhood's intensive research, in dialogue with academic scholars, is an intricate map of the many possible factors that give rise to problematic drug use, to being involved in dealing in drugs, to the impact of drug use on families and communities and to the various options that (ideally) exist to reduce the harm associated with drug use. As a theatrical production *Ulwembu* provides a platform for exploring the vexing emotions and circles of blame that surrounds the use of drugs, particularly at street level.

The production is underpinned by two important sensibilities. The first is 'the more we see drugs, the more we see people'. This means that in the production people for whom drugs have a primary salience are not dispensable non-humans. On the contrary, as the play so brilliantly demonstrates, they are people who have experienced some form of disconnect or trauma in their lives and the drugs are a solution that blunts these feelings. They are thinking, feeling beings who should be awarded the same basic human rights as any other person, including the right to privacy, health care and dignity.

The second sensibility is that coming down hard on people who use drugs – particularly those from low-income backgrounds – does more harm than good. Users become increasingly stigmatised, traumatised and marginalised when a heavy-handed law enforcement approach is used, usually as the first line of action.

Criminal records make finding 'decent' work incredibly difficult and so, as the play brilliantly shows, users become dealers. And dealers, contrary to popular belief, are often not just the 'bad guys'. In some cases they are the only people who are able to hear and make sense of the daily struggles of those who have a drug-use disorder. But beyond this, they are trying to forge a meaningful life for themselves that generates an income, which often benefits extended family members.

A vital lesson that *Ulwembu* teaches us is that it really does not help anyone in this labyrinth of drug use and drug markets to throw blame around. As Mpume Mthombeni, who plays the role of Portia, so aptly states towards the end of the play, blame does not help to deal with drug use and drug markets. In a powerful monologue she says that blame cannot be used, or sold or eaten.

What is needed instead is compassion and an understanding of what pathways are or should be available to those with a drug-use disorder who are keen to normalise their lives and recover from the harmful impact of dependent drug use. We need to take collective responsibility for making sense of problematic drug use and finding solutions that are based on positive personal experiences and on international evidence of best practice harm reduction.

The dialogues and monologues that make *Ulwembu* facilitate deliberation among and between a wide range of social groupings, including people who use drugs, family members, religious leaders, police, government officials, policy-makers and civil society. The dialogue between the actors and the audience, together with the visual represent-ations of real-life characters caught up in the web of drug use, provide insights that generate empathetic responses rather than moralistic and judgemental ones.

The research that constituted the foundation of *Ulwembu*, as well as its performance, and the engagement that resulted from this, directly influenced the establishment of South Africa's first Opioid Substitution Therapy (OST) Demonstration Project, which is located in Durban. The OST Project staff attended the play, which reinforced the empathetic approach that has been built into the project from its inception.

In each of the 50 beneficiaries of the OST Project is a voice that resonates with the characters in the play. The voice given in *Ulwembu* to people who use drugs has played a very important role in advocating for harm-reduction interventions in South Africa, including OST.

As a scholar and a public intellectual, I found working closely with *Ulwembu's* producers, directors and actors a truly remarkable experience. Despite having researched drug use in the field, I was unable to unearth the nuances and deep emotive underpinnings of all those entangled in the world of whoonga use.

The Big Brotherhood actors had a remarkable capacity to reach into the lives of the characters they represented in the production – the users, the police, the dealers, community members and social workers. It was not surprising, therefore, that acting out the stories they had revealed, took a massive emotional toll. In turn, the emotions that were so evident on the stage, and the empathetic way in which each character was depicted, left an indelible mark on my own psyche and on my understanding of how best to research both the everyday and the extraordinary.

Equally important, at a personal level I have come to realise that I can play a role in the creative world and that it is imperative to collaborate with creative artists in making sense of and bringing to the fore narratives and solutions that resonate deeply with our humanity and our need to fix 'wicked' problems.

Monique Marks
Professor and Head of the Urban Futures Centre at the Durban University of Technology
January 2018

Introduction

EMPATHEATRE IN DURBAN, SOUTH AFRICA

Dylan McGarry

Ulwembu is a product of deep friendship and a love affair; an example of what happens when a chosen family of concerned citizens come together to truly listen and empathise with a social problem in its immediate environment.

Since 2014, the Big Brotherhood, a KwaMashu-based theatre company, has been working closely with acclaimed South African playwright Neil Coppen, local actress and ethnographer Mpume Mthombeni and me, an educational sociologist. Together we gathered oral histories of Durbanites and collectively transformed them into a captivating theatrical experience.

We developed an interdisciplinary theatre methodology which we have named Empatheatre, which brings together various forms of forum, documentary, verbatim research and applied theatre models. We hoped that through Empatheatre we would be able to share people's real-life stories to inspire and develop a greater empathy and kindness in spaces where there is conflict or injustice.

Ulwembu casts a wide net. It works in the fields of anthropology, sociology, criminology, health, law enforcement, mental health and, of course, theatre. It specifically shares the many stories of young whoonga (brown heroin) users in Durban and explores the role police and government services (such as health and social development) play in the lives of vulnerable youth in the city.

Whoonga (a concoction of B-grade heroin, rat poison and a variety of other toxic chemical components) has been plaguing KwaZulu-Natal communities for the past decade, yet only attracted public attention in recent years when it appeared in the inner city and surrounding suburbs of Durban. The devastating extent and complexity of the problem has been increasing at an alarming rate.

Government and city officials, non-governmental organisations (NGOs) and other groups have struggled to combine forces and react with the speed and efficiency needed to respond meaningfully to the crisis. Ultimately, as team/family, we wanted to do something to encourage a more humane response to street-level drug use and users, especially since some of the users we met were eight years old and living on the street with a severe heroin addiction.

When we began to look at the problem as a team (with vital mentorship from Professor Monique Marks and Dr Kira Erwin) we could see that treating users as psychologically abnormal was a significant problem. Instead, we began to focus on what was absent – meaningful care for and empathy with users. It was clear that it was necessary for government and civil society groups to establish more dynamic and empathetic forms of exchange and partnership.

The outdated punitive models of control were not only further harming individual users, they were contributing to and sustaining environments of violence in which the use of and trade in illegal substances could further expand. It was clear that we had to bring together policing and public health actors and their resources, with the express purpose of seeking realisable strategies for reducing the harm and associated problems caused by illegal substance use.

There was a clear need to open up the minds and thinking of the police, social workers and health care practitioners to consider drug use as a mental health, not a criminal issue. International research has revealed that connection and care dissolve the risks associated with addiction much more successfully than punishment and criminalisation.

In developing *Ulwembu* we could see how vital empathetically engaging with the reality at every level was. We directly challenged existing policing responses (and policy directives) with regard to street level drug addiction. In South Africa these have tended to focus on operational strategies such as crackdowns, dispersal and heavy-handed law enforcement drives. The police were clearly a group we needed to work with. Inspired by Paulo Frere's 'pedagogy of the oppressed' we realised we also needed to consider the pedagogy of the oppressors.

Firstly, the policing strategies that were operational at the time had been shown to contribute inadvertently to the expansion of the illegal drug economy, a market that is complex, fluid and highly adaptable. Secondly, these actions further marginalised an already vulnerable group by forcing its members into peripheral and uninhabitable spaces, which reduces their ability to access primary health care and other services. Thirdly, negative interactions and experiences with the police tended to result in street-level drug users refusing to make use of public facilities and services for fear of being targeted and victimised again by the police. Fourthly, dispersal strategies tend to spread rather than minimise public health problems associated with street-level drug addiction, and finally, the dominant police responses were also associated with increasing risk behaviour and a redistribution of harm.

While the police we interviewed were aware of the problematic outcomes of their existing strategies, they have failed, on their own, to find alternative and more effective ways of responding to street-level drug users and addicts. We could see that this was not the result of a lack of knowledge on the part of the police but rather the result of their being excluded from solution-oriented networks and from groupings that operate broadly within the sphere of public health.

To make matters worse, the police are often viewed as, and made to be, the first responders to the issue of street-level drug use and addiction, when ideally they should be the last. In our learning on the ground, we discovered that policing should not be seen as the sole response to illegal substance use but rather as one (minor) tool in a broad range of strategic responses and interventions. What was required was a radical rethink of the policing of and health care responses to drug addiction. Such a rethink would situate policing and health care within a harm-reduction framework in a way that articulates positively with the recovery movement of drug users and addicts, which is gaining momentum both nationally and internationally.

And so *Ulwembu* not only had an impact on the 'doing' of the policing of street-level drug addiction but also on broader organisational reform, within police and health care organisations, that results from networked approaches to problem-solving, as well as the promotion of police and health practitioners as knowledge builders.

HOW DID WE DO IT?

Our team spent more than a year 'under cover', interviewing users, dealers, police officers, doctors, social workers, ward councillors, parents, principals, teachers and friends in and around Durban (working more like sociologists than theatre-makers). Through that initial process, we found that there are many ways out of drug use, but they require support from the community as a whole.

Researching a play like this required sensitivity, care and constant psychological debriefing as we dived deeper into the world of street-level drug users and witnessed the harrowing and difficult experiences young people had been through. We had to develop not only safe spaces for conversation and storytelling for those we were learning from, but also for our team and company of actors/writers. We worked as researchers, writers, peer counsellors and then, of course, theatre-makers. During performances the actors would embody the worlds of the people they had met and spoken with directly. They felt and understood the stories they were telling with first-hand empathy. Not only did this add to a richer performance, it also ensured that the stories were told properly and ethically, with deep sensitivity, dignity and compassion.

BRINGING A MOTHER'S LOVE TO POLICING IN DURBAN

The characters in *Ulwembu* were, in many senses, developed to suit the abilities, qualities and confidence levels of the various actor/researchers in the group. As Mpume Mthombeni was the most experienced actress, we knew we would position her as a central character. Her performance as Portia, the policewoman who desperately seeks to balance justice, mercy and empathy, centres the narrative. Portia's character is based on testimonials gathered from Metro Police and South African Police Service officers in Durban and various interviews we had with parents of drug users. This device allowed us to incorporate two strands of research and examine them through the lens of a single character.

As a group, we were frustrated that most theatre productions focus exclusively on the oppressed, while failing to interrogate the role and actions of the oppressor. Portia was our way of including the police narratives we had collected and, in a sense, showing how, when it comes to addiction, the oppressor (police force) can in a relative instant be transformed into the oppressed (a mother trying to save her son from grips of addiction). No one is immune.

For Mpume, the inspiration and core of Portia emerged from her interactions and interviews with a female police colonel and a policewoman who worked in Umlazi.

'I borrowed lots from the colonel, whom I went and spoke with on a few occasions', Mpume recalls. 'She told me her personal stories, which I spun into my character. I also borrowed elements from a policewoman I knew from my neighbourhood, who is a no-nonsense woman who holds her own in a very male-dominated space. She always tells me: 'I'm not scared of dying. If my time comes, my time comes'. 'She faced a very similar problem to Portia's when her niece, who had a whoonga problem, was arrested. She told me that she had to make some very hard professional and personal decisions over this time'.

As Mpume explains, her work devising and portraying the character of Portia gave her a new respect for and empathy with women working within in the Metro Police forces. 'Since creating this character,' she says, 'whenever I see policewomen driving around my neighbourhood arresting people or stopping cars I think about our conversations … I think about what she said about people not respecting policewomen because they are women'.

THE POWER OF A CENTRAL IMAGE

Neil Coppen always likes to work with a significant recurring central image that embodies the essence of the story he is telling in a play. In *Ulwembu*, when we illustrate the painful cramps known as *arosta* that are experienced by whoonga smokers, the image consists of ropes wrapped around a character's torso and pulled by other cast members. As they tighten around the character's waist we experience the pain and anguish of falling deeper into the daily torment of addiction fuelled by the fear of *arosta*.

This graphic image also represents something we discovered – that all the people in a community are interconnected and the pain one user feels will affect many others. This central image of connectivity is why we called the play *Ulwembu* (isiZulu for spider web). If we want to respond to drugs humanely and comprehensively in Durban, we need to understand the interwoven and deeply interconnected nature of the problem.

ENCOURAGING COMPASSION AS OPPOSED TO FEAR

Ulwembu is not merely a play that aims to 'scare' young people away from drugs. The life of a whoonga user is scary enough, there is no need to add to that horror. The production goes beyond intimidating audiences, it reveals the entire world of drug use in the city, creating an engrossing, emotive and honest experience for audiences that speaks to the realities of why people begin to use drugs in the first place.

In the development of the character of Andile, a seemingly hardened street user and '*tsotsi*', we worked carefully to avoid stereotyping and stuck carefully to the stories and direct experiences of users and the daily life of a heroin addict. As Ngcebo Cele, who played the role, explains: 'I really wanted to make sure that Andile never came across as a bad person, even though he is troubled and manipulative … He is also charming, street-smart and desperate. I wanted him to feel like a real human being on that stage'. This attitude was central to the way we dealt with stereotyping and the dangerous myth machine that influences our perceptions of street-level users. As Neil reminds us, 'there are no villains, no baddies in this universe. In our research, the word *survival* came up frequently. Our characters are all trying to survive in a merciless landscape'.

In an interview with journalist Lloyd Gedye, Mpume Mthombeni explained: 'Before, I thought all whoonga addicts were just criminals – people who would mug you and steal your phone, so imagine, now I had to approach these people and talk to them ... You need to think about how you approach the users in a respectful manner'. She says that, in a way, you are asking the user to undress in front of you in telling their story. 'And then you realise these people have never been heard and are crying out for attention. They are so relieved that they can pour out their problems to you'. For Mpume it was important that the users understood that the actors came to them in a 'neutral way'. 'These people have a problem that needs to be supported, not punished'.

EMPATHEATRE IS ABOUT LISTENING

Central to this work was the role of listening, one of the most emancipatory things we could offer. We call it 'giving our attention', and that is exactly what we felt we were there to do; to give those on the frontline of this issue our attention. We became masterful listeners –active, empathetic, embodied listeners. The majority of the people we worked with were extremely vulnerable. We immediately got the sense that the stories they had heard had never been about them, and working in this way shifted that imbalance.

WORKING WITH POLITICAL RIGOUR

The character of Emmanuel, the Mozambican, arrived during the workshopping process, a few weeks later than the others. While conducting one of our scripting workshops, we found ourselves in the midst of violent xenophobic attacks, sparked by a speech made by Zulu King Goodwill Zwelethini. These attacks held the city hostage for two weeks. Several people were killed and many injured in mob violence. At the time the group had been discussing the involvement of foreigners in the local drug trade. Should the foreign character be a dealer? Should we not work hard to subvert these sorts of stereotypes? Might our play help dispel ignorance and the blanket assumptions made about foreigners? Making the Emmanuel character a dealer would only confirm popular opinion and support the xenophobic myth machine already in motion.

Our rehearsal space was located at the Denis Hurley Centre (DHC) in the middle of the city, which became a safe haven for families from other African countries afflicted by the violence. Assisting with the relief effort, and entering into conversations with refugees, exposed our team of actors/researchers to a complex part of the story of street-level drug use that we had previously skimmed over. Despite the fact that we found no evidence to support the common belief that the prevalence of drug trade in Durban correlated directly with the presence of foreign nationals, it was the foreigners who were being driven out of the townships under the pretence that they were dealing whoonga to school children.

The violence spread nationally and culminated in a Somali being set alight in his sphaza shop container and the brutal public murder of Emmanuel Sithole from Mozambique. It was Sithole's story, as recounted in an interview with his wife in a Sunday newspaper, that would form the spine of the Emmanuel character in the play. After reading the interviews with Emmanuel's family, we decided to name our character after him, drawing autobiographical elements from his story and combining them with the testimonials of foreign nationals we had met at the DHC and those living within local communities.

We obtained recordings and translations of the King's controversial speech and resolved to use it in the play in a scene where the Emmanuel character is seen to be listening to the radio. The use of this speech in the production sparked controversy among a few audience members and opened up a useful and generative space for dialogue and exchanges about xenophobia and prejudice. Working with what was emerging from this ongoing crisis meant that we had to be rigorous about how we understood the political, cultural and social elements at play. We were vigilant, remembering that there are no innocent positions, and avoiding romantic idealisation and judgement of any kind.

Our team is also involved in ongoing forums with various players in the city, from the police, to health care, community safety and social workers, academics and other groupings. In January 2016 we performed the show before Parliament and key policymakers. In post-show conversations with the audience a deeply transformative form of learning emerged. We began the process with the goal of responding to the complexities surrounding street-level drug addiction in Durban and found ourselves exploring and tending to myriad sociological, political, economic, cultural, psychological and spiritual realities that, in turn, changed us. What we were seeking to transform – the severe disconnect between street-level drug users and the police and health care workers – began to transform us as individuals and as a 'family' of practice.

We are indebted to the Durban community, who came together in the most extraordinary and unexpected way to help us tell this story; a story that belongs to all of us and one that continues to change and evolve.

IMPACT

In our work, we have seen the extraordinary commitment of several sectors in Durban. Partners from the South African Addiction Medicine Society (SAAMS) and the South African Society of Psychiatrists (SASOP), the Metro Police, the South Coast Recovery Group, TB/HIV Care, the University of Cape Town, the Urban Futures, the Denis Hurley Centre and the South African Depression and Anxiety Group came together in an unprecedented collaborative drive to create the first harm reduction and Opioid Substitution Therapy (OST) programme in the country, which is servicing street-level drug users in the Durban area free of charge.

Ulwembu emerged from a series of discussions, meetings and workshops and, while the play, the performances and discussions after the show contributed a great deal to the drive for an OST programme, it was also the incredible foresight and leadership of Monique Marks at the Urban Futures Centre and Shaun Shelley from TB/HIV Care that inspired the creation of a comprehensive harm reduction package in Durban, particularly for heroin users.

While parts of the comprehensive package of the UN Office on Drugs and Crime and the World Health Organisation are provided by NGOs, particularly TB/HIV

Care, OST has not been provided anywhere in Durban. In addition, users currently targeted for intervention are those who inject drugs and harm reduction programmes should be extended to all people who use drugs.

Neither the *Ulwembu* team nor the wider OST advocacy groups regard harm reduction as antithetical to other processes or philosophies of recovery. Advocacy groups strongly belief there are many routes to recovery, but the various components of the harm reduction package (including OST and the needle and syringe programmes) have proved to be effective in assisting users to live safer, more productive and happier lives. OST, provided in a properly regulated and supervised manner, and combined with the necessary psycho-social support, is internationally accepted as an effective way to reduce morbidity, mortality and overdose rates dramatically. In addition, there is clear evidence that OST does provide the scaffolding for moving away from illicit drug use and its associated behaviour.

RESPONSES

Thanks to the Hillbrow Theatre, we performed the play from 25 - 27 January 2017, and launched a self-published version of the playscript in English and in isiZulu. We invited members of Parliament and other significant organisations, the Minister of Health and the Director of the 'Hawks' (the Directorate for Priority Crime Investigation), whose response was '[w]e should not underestimate how powerful this evening has been for us'. The feedback from key guests were productive and the event was a great success.

Five months later, at the SA Drug Policy Week, held in Cape Town, participants who had been involved in the Hillbrow performance reconvened and are now engaging with the Western Cape High Court, with outcomes to be decided in 2018. The court will be asked to consider loosening up the laws which make it illegal to grow, sell, possess or take various drugs and, more importantly, to support harm reduction programmes in the country.

Glossary and translation

amanzi	water
arosta	The street name for the pains that occur as a side effect of smoking whoonga.
asina-choice	it's a means to an end
blazing	street slang for smoking
cheese boy	overly pampered and groomed. A derisive nickname denoting supposed affluence. It comes from the expression 'he can afford to have cheese on his bread'.
eat-sum-more	Whoonga is often referred to as an 'eat-sum-more', a reference to a popular South African shortbread biscuit. The comparison refers to the notion that once you start, you can't stop.
Ebumnyameni ngibona ifu elimnyama, isisu sidungekile kugijima izinkalankala, kuthi khala inhliziyo ibe ncane alikho icala lomzimba elingabuthwele ubunzima. Amathumbu ayadonseka afuna ukuphuma kulo owami umqala ngithi qala amehlo athi filifili, angizifili kulo owami umzimba usuphenduke isidindi. Ngizothi uma ngikhala ngikhale ngizwiwe ubani, ngoba ebumnyameni ngibona ifu elimnyama.	A dark cloud has settled over me. My intestines writhe and rise up through my neck. My vision blurs, obscured. I am no longer in my body. I melt into nothingness, I am brittle like grass in winter. If I cry who will hear me, a dark cloud has settled over me.

four sgodo	four thousand
goof	slang for whoonga. Refers to being high, eg. 'I'm so gooft'.
gwinyas, amagwinya	deep-fried bread, also known as vetkoek
indlala ibanga ulaka	hunger breeds anger. During our research a drug user described how the 'hunger' for whoonga made him so desperate he would resort to anything to get hold of his next hit, even violence if needed. Traditionally, this idiom refers to poverty leading to violence.
intombi engaliwa	another street name for whoonga. Directly translated it means 'a lover you cannot leave'.
iqaqa alizizwa ukunuka	no polecat ever smells its own stink
isangoma	traditional herbalist/healer
iscefe	a nuisance
ishandapha	Zulu street slang for sexy
isigebengu/ isgebengu	robber/gangster
isikhwebu	directly translated, *isikhwebu* refers to maize meal. A colloquialism referring to the fact that everything is for sale, and anything can be turned into money. Used as slang among whoonga users.
izandla ziyagezana	It takes both hands to wash. Equivalent to 'you scratch my back, I'll scratch yours.
kunjani namhlanje	how are you today?
kwerekwere	derogatory term for a foreigner

GLOSSARY AND TRANSLATION

Malume/Umalume	Uncle. Referring to another man as uncle (specifically a maternal uncle), it is a term of respect, the equivalent of Sir.
Ngiyabonga	thank you
njengamanje!	Right now!
iphara	slang derogatory abbreviation for a street-level user, para as in 'parasite'
sjambok	whip made from recycled melted plastic
skhotheni (uskhotheni)	a junkie or 'good-for-nothing'
slagin'	selling
straws	street slang for a type of whoonga sold in plastic drinking straws
thula wena	be quiet/still
trappin'	dealing
uBokodowayo	a traditional isiZulu herbal medicine – a particular type of 'umuti'
uMa ngala ungibangela	My mother was giving me hell.
umziko, khethe, straw	alternative names for whoonga
umfana	boy
umfana wami	my boy
umshana	my friend or comrade
umuthi	traditional medicines created and administered by traditional herbalists and healers (sangomas)
Ungaliyisa ihhashi emfuleni, kodwa ngeke uliphoqe ukuthi liphuze	You can take a horse to the river but you can't make him drink.

uyafuqa!	you eat till you're stuffed
uyinja	you dog
voetsak	Afrikaans word meaning piss off/get out of here/get lost
wangigabha	literally, a lot of bottle; slang meaning 'she left me'

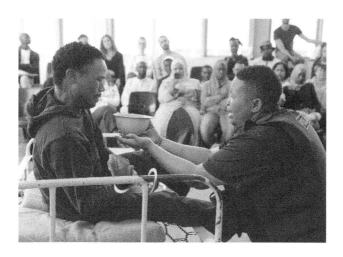

PORTIA (Mpume Mthombeni) attempts to get her son SIPHO (Zenzo Msomi) to eat. Photograph by Val Adamson.

SIPHO (Zenzo Msomi) embodying the painful cramps known as 'Arosta'. Photograph by Val Adamson.

Above and below: Policewoman PORTIA MTHEMBU (Mpume Mthombeni) interrogates drug runner ANDILE (Ngcebo Cele). Photographs by Val Adamson.

EMMANUEL (Sandile Nxumalo) listens in horror to King Goodwill Zwelethini's xenophobic speech. Photograph by Val Adamson.

BONGANI (Vumani Khumalo) threatens ANDILE (Ngcebo Cele). Photograph by Val Adamson.

SIZWE (Zenzo Msomi) begs ANDILE (Ngcebo Cele) to help him quit smoking whoonga. Photograph by Val Adamson.

SIPHO (Zenzo Msomi) discovers the body of ANDILE (Ngcebo Cele). Photograph by Val Adamson.

Ulwembu

CHARACTERS

LIEUTENANT PORTIA MTHEMBU … A 46-year-old policewoman in KwaMashu

SIPHO MTHEMBU … Portia's 16-year-old son, an aspiring poet and songwriter

BONGANI MSELEKU … A 30-year-old dealer in KwaMashu[1]

ANDILE NXUMALO … A 16-year-old whoonga user and friend of Sipho

EMMANUEL ABREU … A 35-year-old sphaza shop owner from Mozambique[2]

POLICE CHIEF … A 50-year-old jaded officer

Actors playing POLICE CHIEF, Bongani and Emmanuel, double in smaller cameo roles of social worker, sangoma, additional policeman, and so on.

Ulwembu previewed at the Inanda Theatre Festival in Durban in March 2015. It went on to play at universities, community centres, festivals and schools and enjoyed a long run at the Durban Playhouse Loft Theatre in April 2016. In 2017 it had a limited run at the Hillbrow Theatre in Johannesburg to an audience that included several members of Parliament at a special performance aimed at influencing South Africa's policy on harm-reduction support.

Portia was played by Mpume Mthombeni, Sipho by Zenzo Msomi, Bongani/social worker/policeman by Vumani Khumalo, Andile by Ngcebo Cele, Emmanuel/Zikhali/

Isangoma by Sandile Nxumalo and the Police Chief/
Bulawayo by Phumlani Ngubane.

*The set consists of three distinct colours: black, white and
red. The staging should work in traditional theatre spaces
as well as within informal public spaces. The boundaries of
the Ulwembu world are formed by six identical black or red
chairs, four in each corner and the fifth and sixth on the left
and right sides of the stage. A single hospital bed at the back
of the stage stands with the headboard pointing upward so
that the spring mesh resembles a barbed wire fence. Four
red plastic crates (containing key props/wardrobe changes)
sit beside the four corner chairs. All props and costumes
are either black, red or white. Two parallel red ropes (each
5m long) are placed up and downstage. No wings are used
during scenes. When cast members are not involved in a
scene they occupy the four corner chairs, serving as silent
witnesses to events. Between scenes the actors who have
been seated move in carefully choreographed slow motion,
preparing costumes and props for the next scene. The play is
performed in isiZulu and English, with the ratios adjusted
according to the demographics of the audience.*

Prologue

OUR STORY

Six chairs form a circle on the stage. Portia stands a little hesitantly at the centre, with Sipho sitting beside her. The rest of the cast occupy the remaining chairs. PORTIA *addresses the room.*

PORTIA: For weeks I've sat in this support group, afraid of that moment when I would be asked to step forward and tell our story. [*Pause.*]Before I joined this group it felt like I was alone in the world … that no one would understand. How could they? As a mother, I felt ashamed, that this was all my fault; that I had failed. It is only through all of your courage that I have come to realise that we all turn to things to numb the pain, to distract ourselves from our deepest fears. [*Pause.*] My name is Portia Mthembu and I'm ready now to tell my story.

Blackout.

Scene 1

BEHIND THE POLICE STATION

The wail of police sirens, flashing of red and blue lights.
ANDILE, *wearing a black hoodie that conceals his face comes hurtling through the audience and onto the stage.*

PORTIA [*yelling from audience*]: You run, I shoot. Do you hear me? You hear me?

> *Torch beams scan the darkness as members of the Metro Police arrive on stage.* PORTIA, *a sturdy policewoman of around 40, wearing a bulletproof jacket, leads the chase.*

> ANDILE *is trapped. He stops out of breath as* PORTIA, *flanked by the rest of her unit [including* officers BULAWAYO *and* ZIKHALI] *surround him.*

PORTIA: I will pull this trigger. I will shoot.

> ANDILE *tries to dash but is pushed forcefully down to the ground by* ZIKHALI.

BULAWAYO: Get down on the ground.
PORTIA: On the ground. Do you hear me?

> PORTIA *pins* ANDILE *to the floor, securing his hands behind his head. She inspects his face with the flashlight.*

PORTIA: You … again?
ANDILE *grimaces.*
PORTIA: Ayanda?

4

ANDILE: Andile.

> ANDILE *tries to wriggle free but* PORTIA *shoves him back down.*

PORTIA: How could I forget? What have we got today, eh?

ZIKHALI: Empty your pockets.

ANDILE: Please, Lieutenant.

PORTIA: Don't waste our time boy.

ANDILE: I have nothing on me.

PORTIA: I'm a busy woman. Empty them.

ANDILE: Please …

PORTIA [*assertive*]: Empty your pockets.

ANDILE: Just let me go … please.

PORTIA: Would you like Captain Bulawayo to empty them for you? Do you remember what happened the last time Officer Bulawayo had to empty them for you? [*Calling.*] Bulawayo!

BULAWAYO [*stepping forward*]: I am here, Lieutenant.

PORTIA: You remember Officer Bulawayo, Andile?

ANDILE [*stammering*]: I remember.

PORTIA: And Officer Zikhali?

ANDILE: Yes, Ma.

PORTIA: I would like to make this quick and easy for all of us this evening. Empty your pockets.

> ANDILE *empties his pockets. A few ziplock bags filled with whoonga straws fall to the ground.*

ANDILE: Please Ma, please let me keep my *goof*.

PORTIA: Allow you to pollute all the other children in this community? You want me to arrest you again? How many times has it been this month? [*No answer.*] You can't remember, eh? Zikhali, can you?

ZIKHALI: I think five, Lieutenant.

PORTIA [*shaking her head*]: And for what? For this nonsense? [*She holds the packet of whoonga straws in front of his face.*] Where are you getting these? Where?

ANDILE *doesn't answer.*

PORTIA: Where are you getting these from, Andile?

BULAWAYO: Answer the question boy. Where?

ZIKHALI: Make him talk, Bulawayo.

> ANDILE *doesn't answer.* BULAWAYO *hits him in the stomach.* ANDILE *collapses, moaning.*

BULAWAYO: Where are you getting this stuff from, eh? Who is your dealer?

PORTIA: I'm running out of ideas.

ZIKHALI: Let's teach him a lesson.

PORTIA: The days of all that paperwork and fingerprinting at the station are over.

ANDILE: Please, Lieutenant, let me keep my *goof.* I will starve if I can't sell it.

BULAWAYO: Did you hear that? Shame, this boy must be hungry.

ZIKHALI: Let's make him eat it, Lieutenant.

BULAWAYO: Ja, eat it.

PORTIA [*concerned*]: Eat it?

ANDILE [*begging from the ground*]: Please no ... please, Lieutenant.

BULAWAYO: Quiet.

ANDILE: Please ...

BULAWAYO: Destroy the evidence so we can all just move

along. [*Beat.*] Eat it, boy.
PORTIA [*a little concerned*]: It won't hurt him?
ANDILE: It's too much. [*Begging.*] Please.
BULAWAYO: He must learn. EAT IT!
PORTIA: Listen to the officer, Andile …
ZIKHALI: Eat it!

> BULAWAYO *and two other officers grab* ANDILE *and force some of the contents of the bags into his mouth. He lets out a cry, followed by silence. The scene freezes.* PORTIA *steps out of it, holding a torch to her face, and addresses the audience.*

PORTIA: Have we lost our humanity? That's what you're thinking, isn't it? It's easy for you to sit there and judge me and my colleagues? This is the twelfth youngster we have had to reprimand like this tonight, and I can guarantee you there will be a hundred or so by the end of the week. I saw this kid arrive in our neighbourhood at the beginning of the year. [*Pause.*] Watched his habit grow out of control. It's gotten so bad that even at funerals things go missing. [*Beat. She glances over at* ANDILE *with disgust.*] How can I have sympathy for a boy who steals wedding rings off corpses' fingers at family funerals? [*She shakes her head.*]

> *We snap back to the scene.*

BULAWAYO: Now the other one.
ANDILE: I can't … Please …
ZIKHALI: You heard us.

ANDILE *empties the second and third straws into his mouth.*

BULAWAYO: Swallow.

ANDILE *shakes his head.*

ZIKHALI: You heard the officer. Swallow.

ANDILE *gulps it down, gagging.*

PORTIA: He needs water.

BULAWAYO: He'll be fine.

ZIKHALI: Chew boy … chew.

PORTIA: Someone give him water. [*No response.* ANDILE *coughs.* PORTIA *looks at* ZIKHALI.] Zikhali! *Amanzi.*

ZIKHALI *brings a bottle of water and tosses it towards* ANDILE, *who washes the substance down.*

PORTIA: Go back to school, boy. You hear me?

BULAWAYO: Let's put him in the van … drop him somewhere down the South Coast.

PORTIA: Ai! It's a waste of time … these *isigebengu* are like dogs … you can take them way out past the freeway, and by the morning they are at your front door begging for scraps.

THE POLICE *disperse, leaving* ANDILE *in a heap on the floor.*

Scene 2

THE POLICE STATION, CAPTAIN'S OFFICE

PORTIA *wearily takes a seat in front of the* CAPTAIN *of the station.*

CAPTAIN: Do you have any news for me, Lieutenant?

PORTIA: News?

CAPTAIN: The press keep calling for a comment.

PORTIA: We're getting closer, Captain.

CAPTAIN: Closer?

PORTIA: To the dealers, Captain.

CAPTAIN: Closer is not quite the comment I am looking for Lieutenant. [*Pause.*] The media are calling it the Whoonga Apocalypse. [*Pause.*] The reputation of this station is at an all-time low.

PORTIA: We're chasing some new leads.

CAPTAIN [*strongly*]: I need some good news, Lieutenant.[3]

PORTIA: Don't we all, Captain!

CAPTAIN: I need some high-profile arrests for the front pages. Something to put the community at ease.

PORTIA: These things take time, Captain.

CAPTAIN: We don't have time on our side, Lieutenant. [*Pause.*] There are more addicts each and every day out there on our streets and what does that do for crime … the economy? It's a far reaching catastrophe this. [*Pause.*] Our children are no longer safe.

Scene 3

THE SCHOOLYARD

SIPHO, *in school uniform, enters and sits alone.* ANDILE, *also in school uniform, enters and takes a seat beside him.*

ANDILE: Hey *Cheese boy*, why you looking so sad today?

SIPHO *shrugs.*

ANDILE: Girl troubles?

SIPHO: How'd you know?

ANDILE: I always used to see you hanging out with that girl from Grade 10.

SIPHO [*exasperated*]: Ja, Simphiwe.

ANDILE: She was *fresh, yellow-bone, ishandapha*! What happened?

SIPHO: She met someone else.

ANDILE: Those sugar daddies have all the fun.

SIPHO: *Wangigabha.* She told me about him yesterday.

ANDILE: How's your heart, *mfana*?

SIPHO: Ai, it's heavy, bra. [*Pause.* SIPHO *looks at* ANDILE.] Where have you been? I haven't seen you around school for a while.

ANDILE: I had some business to take care of.

SIPHO: What kind of business?

ANDILE: Just some sales.

SIPHO: What you *slagin'*?

ANDILE: Ah Cheese boy, you ask a lot of questions, hey.

SIPHO: My friend Themba says that you are *trappin'*.

ANDILE [*laughing*]: Is that what Themba says?

SIPHO: Ja, he says you sell from behind Emmanuel's store, after school.

ANDILE: Sell what?

SIPHO: Whoonga.

ANDILE [*unconvincingly*]: Na, he must have me confused with someone else. I'm innocent.

SIPHO: He says you are blazing as well, says that's why you always fall asleep in class.

ANDILE: Why are you so interested? [*Pause.*] You ever tried it?

SIPHO: Tried what?

ANDILE: To smoke …

SIPHO: Cigarettes?

ANDILE: No … umziko, khethe, straw?

SIPHO: No.

ANDILE: I bet you'd like it.

SIPHO: You think so?

ANDILE: I don't think so, I know so! That heaviness you speak of. That pain in your heart. You can make it go away. I had it too, Cheese boy. When I was in Jozi my girl of three years left me. Three years! I was going mad without her. *UMa ngala ungibangela iscefe,* the teachers at school, complaining about my grades. I was in trouble with the blue uniform. The world felt like it was pushing down on me. [*Pause.*] My friend Zorro brought some to school one day. [*Pause.*] A few puffs and none of it mattered anymore. I was hovering above everything. It's like you're floating … floating above all the hurt and pain. I was the owner of the whole territory, man. [*Beat.*] Tomorrow you should come with me.

SIPHO: Where to?

ANDILE: We'll go on an adventure. Get out of this prison. Come with me to paradise, Cheese boy. All you have to do is say yes … come on.

SIPHO: I don't think that …

ANDILE: Come on.

SIPHO: I have an essay due …

ANDILE: Cheese boy, leave the rest up to me. [*Pause.*] Just say yes?

SIPHO *hesitates.*

SIPHO: Okay.

Scene 4

PORTIA'S HOUSE

SIPHO *is sitting on the sofa watching television.* PORTIA
*sneaks up behind him and conceals a package behind his
chair.*

PORTIA: How are you, my boy?

SIPHO: I'm not a boy anymore, Ma.

PORTIA: You're right, you're a big man now. [*Pause.*]
　　　17 years … today?

SIPHO [*annoyed*]: 16 … yesterday.

PORTIA: Yesterday? Happy Birthday.

SIPHO: You forgot!

PORTIA [*wearily*]: When you work so many night shifts in a
　　　row you lose track of what day it is. I'm tired.

SIPHO: I'm tired too …

PORTIA: They're putting pressure on me at the station.
　　　[*Pause.*]

SIPHO: Tired of hearing how tired you are, Ma.

PORTIA: Rub your mamma's shoulders?

SIPHO: No, Ma.

PORTIA: I've been running after *tsotsis* all week. That
　　　bulletproof vest has been hurting my shoulders.

SIPHO: Does this mean I get a raise in my pocket money?

PORTIA: R10.

SIPHO: R20.

PORTIA: R20!!!

SIPHO: And you pay upfront.

PORTIA: Upfront? [*She removes her purse and gives*

13

him R20.] Come … come. [*She pats her shoulders impatiently.* SIPHO *starts to massage them.*] How is school going?

SIPHO: Ma, I don't want to go back to school anymore … it's a waste of time.

PORTIA: But you are doing so well. *Usufuna ukuba uskhotheni, uhlale ema-tuckshop ufuqa amagwinya?* [You want to be a *skhotheni* hanging around the tuck shop eating *gwinyas* all day?]

SIPHO: No Ma, I want to be a musician. They are not teaching me anything that interests me.

SIPHO *squeezes* PORTIA's *shoulders a bit too hard.*

PORTIA: Ai! Gentle *umfana wami.* Did you make us some dinner?

SIPHO: There was nothing in the fridge.

PORTIA: Nothing? Shall I make us a sandwich?

SIPHO: There's no bread.

PORTIA [*confused*]: But I went shopping …

SIPHO: A week ago! [*Pause.*] I'm a growing man.

PORTIA [*laughing*]: Ja, *uyafuqa!* With a grown-man's appetite. I'll take you out on my next night off, nê? We'll go to a restaurant to celebrate properly. [PORTIA *remembers the packet she arrived with.*] You really thought I forgot? I want you to open it.

SIPHO *opens a box and reveals a pair of expensive looking red sneakers.*

PORTIA: These are the ones you wanted, nê?

SIPHO [*excitedly*]: Yes!

SIPHO *slips them on to his feet*

PORTIA: Do they fit?

SIPHO: Thank you!

PORTIA [*remembering*]: I want you to have this.

> PORTIA *removes a chain with a gold wedding ring on it from her pocket and hangs it around* SIPHO's *neck.*

PORTIA: This was the wedding ring your father gave me. He saved up for two years to be able to buy it. [*Pause.*] The day he was killed on duty was the same day I learnt I was pregnant with you. [*She touches his face tenderly.*] I see so much of him in you. He would have been so proud of you. [*Referring to the chain.*] I want you to keep this close to you. Keep it close to your heart.

> *Lights fade. The acappella hymn 'Somebody' by the King's Messengers Quartet begins.*

Scene 5

BEHIND EMMANUEL'S SPHAZA SHOP

The song continues in this scene as ANDILE *and* SIPHO, *still in school uniform, enter. They look around cautiously before* ANDILE *sits on the bench and sets about rolling a whoonga spliff. He lights it and takes a drag before passing it to* SIPHO. *As* SIPHO *takes his first drag the hymn recedes into the distance and is replaced by a gritty, surreal soundscape.*

The two sit back to back in the aftermath, hazy from the drug. Finally, SIPHO *musters the strength to speak.*

SIPHO: I want to feel that feeling again.

ANDILE: That can be arranged.

SIPHO: When?

ANDILE: You can meet me behind this *kwerekwere* sphaza shop after school.

SIPHO: His name's Emmanuel. [*Pause.*] I can't wait that long.

ANDILE [*producing a packet of whoonga*]: I'm going to give you a present, bra. It's two days' worth of *goof*.

SIPHO: Two days?

ANDILE: Ja. You going to need to this to help you through the nights.

SIPHO: How much will it cost me?

ANDILE: The first stash is free.

SIPHO: Ai … Ai … free? What's the catch?

ANDILE: From now onwards I'm your dealer, you only ever buy from me?

SIPHO: Okay. I'm down with that.

ANDILE: That's my boy!

Scene 6

BEHIND EMMANUEL'S SPHAZA SHOP

EMMANUEL *enters, wielding a sjambok.*

EMMANUEL: Ai, what's going on here? Shouldn't you two
>   boys be in school? You, [*pointing to* ANDILE.] I've told
>   you before you can't hang around here killing yourself
>   with this rat poison. You are giving my sphaza shop a
>   bad name! Must I call the police again, eh?

ANDILE [*indifferent*]: Do what you like. I'm not afraid
>   of you or the police, *kwerekwere*! Maybe it's me
>   that should be calling the police, so they can come
>   check if you have a permit to be working here in our
>   territory, eh? If you don't like it then just go back to
>   Mozambique.

SIPHO: Stop it, Andile.

ANDILE: Go back to where you came from.

SIPHO: Stop it! Emmanuel is my friend.

> EMMANUEL *recognises* SIPHO, *who lies slumped on the floor.*

EMMANUEL: Sipho?

> SIPHO *smiles.* EMMANUEL *attempts to help him to his feet.*

EMMANUEL [*sternly*]: What are you doing hanging with
>   this *isigebengu* eh, Sipho? What would your mother
>   say if she found out?

SIPHO [*goofl*]: Please don't tell her. Please bra, Emmanuel.
>   We are just having a little fun.

EMMANUEL: He's bad news this Andile. [SIPHO *stares*

blankly at him.] And you're a bright young man. [*He glares at* ANDILE.] I've seen this one destroy far too many young lives. [*To* ANDILE, *maybe even handling him physically.*] I don't want to see you here again. Do you hear me? [ANDILE *runs off.*] You can't go back to school or home looking like this. You must wait here until you've cleaned up. This is the last time this happens boy.

SIPHO: Yes Emmanuel.

EMMANUEL: The last time!

Scene 7

THE POLICE STATION

PORTIA *is once again attending a briefing in the* CAPTAIN'*s office.*

CAPTAIN: Lieutenant Mthembu.

PORTIA: Captain.

CAPTAIN: Do you have any headlines for me yet?

PORTIA: Nothing worth hanging on a lamppost, Captain. My guys are working towards a bust …

CAPTAIN: I'm doing a press briefing at the end of this week. I'm going to need them to work harder.

PORTIA: We are moving as fast as we can.

CAPTAIN: May I ask why you and your team keep wasting your time with the small fish … the *skhotheni* at the bottom, eh? Don't you think it's time you started clamping down on the big boys at the top?

PORTIA: It's only through the runners and dealers at the bottom that we are able to find out who and where the big boys are hiding. These guys are almost impossible to get to.

CAPTAIN: What about intelligence?

PORTIA: Intelligence is working on it but, like I said, it's a slow process.

CAPTAIN: The public are losing confidence in us. You just have to listen to any radio show or read any newspaper to hear what the word on the street is.

PORTIA: I didn't enter this profession to win a popularity contest, Captain.

CAPTAIN: They're saying we can't be trusted … that we are all corrupt … that the dealers have bribed us to keep out of their way. The communities are tired of being robbed.

PORTIA: So am I, Captain.

CAPTAIN: It seems you and your team needs to look at revising your strategies.

PORTIA: The more I deal with this problem, Captain, the more I feel the way we *police* these issues needs to be revised all together.

CAPTAIN: Do you have any suggestions?

PORTIA: We are understaffed and underqualified. We need training, specialised teams. This isn't something we can solve as a single police station … we need help from the top … help from the community. Government need to step in. [*Pause.*] From my experience down on the ground, arresting these users just seems to be making it worse.

She exits.

Scene 8

EMMANUEL'S SPHAZA SHOP

PORTIA *is paying for some groceries.* EMMANUEL *stands on the opposite side of the counter. They greet each other warmly, as if they are old friends.*

EMMANUEL: Good afternoon, Lieutenant.

PORTIA: Bon dia, Emmanuel.

EMMANUEL [*speaking carefully in basic isiZulu*]: *Kunjani namhlanje?*

PORTIA: Your Zulu is getting good! Some bread and R12 Vodacom, please. [*Pause.*] How are you keeping?

EMMANUEL: Things are okay.

PORTIA: You look worried.

EMMANUEL: People came round here this morning and threatened me in my shop.

PORTIA: Again?

EMMANUEL: Ai! I am not sleeping anymore.

PORTIA: Is it the same people as before?

EMMANUEL: It's hard to say who. It's hard to know who to trust anymore in this community. The other night after I had locked up they broke in here and stole all my stock.

PORTIA: Again?

EMMANUEL: Ja.

PORTIA: I am sorry to hear this, Emmanuel.

EMMANUEL: They accuse me of dealing drugs to youngsters but I am no dealer, Portia. I make an honest living with my shop. [*Pause.*] You know if it was up to me

I would pack up and go home tomorrow. I miss my village in Beira and my wife and children. I don't feel welcome here anymore.

PORTIA: I will look out for you. Let me know if you are not feeling safe?

EMMANUEL [*calling after her a little anxiously*]: Portia, sorry Portia, would you mind transferring this money back home to my wife Selina for me again? I'm sorry to ask but it's the end of the month now.

EMMANUEL *holds out a brown envelope.*

PORTIA: I will do it on Monday. [*She takes the envelope.*] Stay safe Emmanuel.

EMMANUEL: God bless you, Portia, *ngiyabonga.*

Scene 9

OUTSIDE EMMANUEL'S SPHAZA SHOP

PORTIA *turns to leave and collides with* BONGANI, *who is entering the store. Her groceries scatter on the ground.* BONGANI *apologises profusely and crouches down to help her pick them up.*

BONGANI: I'm sorry, Ma.
PORTIA: That's okay.

   A moment of recognition as they scan each other's faces.

PORTIA: I know you …
BONGANI: Bongani.
PORTIA: Mseleku … Bongani Mseleku.
BONGANI [*bitterly*]: You have a good memory.
PORTIA: How could I forget? It's been a while?
BONGANI: Four years.
PORTIA: I trust you're enjoying your new-found freedom.
BONGANI: Four years.
PORTIA: That's a long time.
BONGANI: You stole four years of my life.
PORTIA: You brought it upon yourself.
BONGANI: Left me with a criminal record.
PORTIA: You and your friends destroyed a young girl's life.
BONGANI: I didn't lay a hand on her, Officer.
PORTIA [*a little smugly*]: I'm a lieutenant now.

   They stare at each other for a moment.

BONGANI: Do you know how hard it is to find a job with a criminal record? To run a household, feeding three children, when you can't find a job?

PORTIA: The court made the decision in the end.

BONGANI: I was innocent!

PORTIA: That's not what they found, Bongani.

BONGANI: You ruined my life, Lieutenant.

PORTIA: You reap what you sow. [*Beat.*] *Uvuna okutshalile.*

PORTIA *exits.*

Scene 10

OUTSIDE EMMANUEL'S SPHAZA SHOP

SIPHO *is lying on the floor clutching his belly, writhing in terrible pain.*

SIPHO: Andile help me, please … help me. I'm dying from the stomach pain here. It hurts … it hurts so much.

ANDILE: *Arosta.[4]*

SIPHO: Ar … what?

ANDILE: *Arosta.* It's part of the come down.

SIPHO: What's causing this?

ANDILE: The rat poison in the *goof.*

SIPHO: What?

ANDILE: The rat poison leaving your system.

SIPHO: You never told me we were blazing *rat poison*!

ANDILE: The drug would kill us if we smoked it clean. The *rattex* is part of the mix … it keeps the blood flowing.

SIPHO: How can I make it stop?

ANDILE: There's only one way, my bra.

SIPHO [*desperate*]: Tell me what it is … tell me.

ANDILE: You have to smoke more.

SIPHO: More?

ANDILE: It's the only way.

SIPHO: Do you have any more on you?

ANDILE: Of course.

SIPHO: Let's blaze.

ANDILE: Not so fast, Cheese boy … you're going to have to pay up from now on. R25 bucks a hit. That's four hits for R100. That should keep you going for the rest of the day.

SIPHO: What about the rest of the week?

ANDILE: You going to have to find the cash for that.

SIPHO: I don't have any money.

ANDILE: That's not my problem, bra.

SIPHO: Ai Andile, help a friend out.

ANDILE: I'm not a charity, Cheese boy.

SIPHO [*begging*]: Please.

ANDILE: This is my business. My boss will kill me. You have
to pay upfront from now on.

SIPHO: I don't have cash on me.

Pause.

ANDILE [*glancing down at the new sneakers* SIPHO *is
wearing*]: What about those?

SIPHO: These were a birthday present.

ANDILE: I'll give you a week's supply.

SIPHO: *Ai, voetsak!* Once I get rid of this pain then I'm
going to stop smoking this shit forever.

SIPHO *takes off his shoes and throws them angrily at*
ANDILE, *who collects his prize and examines them.*
ANDILE *laughs.*

SIPHO: What's so funny?

ANDILE: Ha! You think you can turn your back on
whoonga just like that?

SIPHO [*clutching his stomach*]: Hurry up with that *blaze*
man.

ANDILE: Your blood is dirty now, Sipho. You smoke once
… twice … three times and you're fucked! That's why
they call this *intombi engaliwa.*

He lights the joint for SIPHO *and hands it to him.* SIPHO *smokes.*

SIPHO: You'll see. I'll give her up.

ANDILE: Not before she steals your cash … breaks your heart … and leaves you in a gutter.

SIPHO: I'm not weak like you, Andile.

ANDILE: Every morning I wake up and say: 'No more … today I am I'm done with this.'

SIPHO: I have my whole life ahead of me.

ANDILE: That's what we all say.

SIPHO: I'll do it!

ANDILE: You think you'll be able to ignore it …

SIPHO: You'll see.

ANDILE: … you think that the pain will just go away? No, it will only get worse, this is an eat-sum-more!

ANDILE *rises and begins to rap in Zulu. Music underscores the sequence.*

ANDILE: *Ebumnyameni ngibona ifu elimnyama, isisu sidungekile kugijima izinkalankala, kuthi khala inhliziyo ibe ncane. Alikho icala lomzimba elingabuthwele ubunzima. Amathumbu ayadonseka afuna ukuphuma kulo owami umqala ngithi qala amehlo athi filifili, angizifili kulo owami umzimba usuphenduke isidindi. Ngizothi uma ngikhala ngikhale ngizwiwe ubani, ngoba ebumnyameni ngibona ifu elimnyama.*

THE COMPANY, *wearing balaclavas, slowly enters the stage and circles ominously around* ANDILE, *wrapping long pieces of rope around his belly before moving to positions on opposite corners of the stage. As their grip gradually tightens the ropes fasten painfully around* ANDILE*'s stomach.* SIPHO *looks on.*

ANDILE [*grimacing*]: And you find that all you can think about is *intombi, intombi, intombi engaliwa.* And soon you realise that nothing will make the pain go away except … smoking more.

ANDILE *takes the joint and inhales with desperation. The ropes relax and slacken around his stomach, falling to the ground. He is overcome with relief.*

ANDILE: But whoonga costs money, nê? It doesn't just grow on trees. So first you pay R25 for one hit. In the beginning you need one hit a day but as your body gets more and more used to it you start to need two and the next week … four. And soon 25 bucks becomes 50, then 100, until finally you have to find R150 bucks a day to fund your *goof.*

SIPHO: Where the fuck am I going to find R150 a day?

ANDILE: The user always makes a plan *mfana.* It's all about the hustle, my bra. [*He strikes a pose.*] Allow me to introduce you to Andile Nxumalo's survival guide to ensure you remain well and truly *gooft* in KwaZulu-Natal in the twenty first century. [ANDILE *mimes the actions of the next sequence, bringing them to life with comic flair.*] There are many ways you may choose to source this sort of income such as … [*Pause.*] working as a caddie there by Greyville golf course on Saturdays …

SIPHO: I don't know anything about golf.

ANDILE: Ai, relax boy. All you have to do is carry the clubs around for the *gqonqa*, who are too lazy to do it themselves. Smile at the *Baas* politely and always congratulate him after each shot … saying things like [*Putting on an accent.*] 'What brilliant aim you have, Sir!' or 'Excellent shot!'.

They get tipped and blaze up.

ANDILE: Or you can help carry the *gogo's* groceries at the Bridge City Mall. [*They re-enact the scene.*] Be polite … greet them warmly … remind them of their favourite grandson. Tell them you are saving up to invest in your university education for when you graduate from high school. [*Pause.*] Although there is always the point where you come short. This is where you going to need to start taking some chances *umshana*.

SIPHO: How do you mean?

ANDILE: When I first started smoking whoonga, I used to steal meat from the delivery truck at the stop street and then sell it to people in the township for half the price.

SIPHO: You mean breaking the law?

ANDILE: When your stash is running low … that, my friend, is when you need to have a 'quick-fix' emergency plan.

SIPHO: Emergency plan?

ANDILE: It is at *this* point that I should tell you about what is known by the user as '*isikhwebu*' … I'm talking minimum effort for a maximum high. Everything you see around us can be transformed into quick cash and more *goof*.

SIPHO: Isikhwebu?

ANDILE [*playfully listing options for theft in a kind of rhyme*]: Sound systems, Playstations, medication,

copper wire, hairdryers, hair extensions, not to
mention ... [*Pause.*] iPhones, iPads, Samsungs,
handguns, hubcaps, wedding rings and other bling.
[*Pause.*] Suitcases, shoelaces, cricket bats, chicken
fat. [*Pause.*] Leather boots, pots 'n pans, bicycles,
Coke cans, wall fans, nail polish, gold teeth, those
silk sheets, Gqonqa's leather-wallets, you know ...
something fancy... like your sister's panties ...

ANDILE *gets higher and higher as he points out all
the possibilities for financing his habit and eventually
collapses to the floor with* SIPHO.

ANDILE [*laughing deliriously*]: Soon you won't care if it's
your own mother you are stealing from ...

PORTIA *calls frantically for* SIPHO *from off stage.*
ANDILE *vanishes.*

Scene 11

PORTIA'S HOUSE

PORTIA *enters and confronts* SIPHO.

PORTIA: Sipho … Sipho!!!

SIPHO: What's wrong?

PORTIA: These thieves have ransacked the house again.

SIPHO: What happened?

PORTIA: They must have broken in last night.

SIPHO: What makes you think that?

PORTIA: The toaster and kettle are gone and that envelope of money I am supposed to be sending home for Emmanuel has gone missing.

SIPHO: Serious, Ma?

PORTIA: What I can't understand is that there's no sign of breaking in and entering.

SIPHO: Someone must have left the door unlocked.

PORTIA: You were the last one home last night. Did you forget to lock when you came in?

SIPHO: I … I might have. I had soccer practice … went out with friends afterwards.

PORTIA: I tried to call. [*Pause.*] Why haven't you been answering my calls or SMSs?

SIPHO: My phone was stolen.

PORTIA: When?

SIPHO: About a week ago … at school.

PORTIA [*concerned*]: And you only tell me now.

SIPHO: I thought I'd told you already.

PORTIA [*looking at her son suspiciously*]: Sipho …

SIPHO *turns away to avoid further scrutiny.* PORTIA *takes his face in her hands and turns him towards her again.*

PORTIA: Are you okay, my boy?

SIPHO: I'm fine, Ma.

PORTIA: You look ...

SIPHO: Tired, I'm just tired.

PORTIA: Is that all?

SIPHO *nods.*

PORTIA: This neighbourhood is under attack. We have to keep things locked at all times. These *skoteni* will steal the sheets off us while we sleeping if we not careful. Ai! I'm fed up with this now ... fed up.

They both exit.

Scene 12

BONGANI'S HOUSE

BONGANI *throws* ANDILE *onto the stage and paces furiously after him, waving a handful of cash in his face.*

BONGANI: This isn't enough.

ANDILE: It's all there, bra.

BONGANI: I gave you four thousand rands worth of stock last week to sell and you giving me two thousand back. [*Aggressively.*] Come … where's the rest of my money?

ANDILE: Ai, just chillax … there was *four sgodo* there when I last checked.

BONGANI: Would you like me to count it again for you? Eh?

ANDILE: That won't be necessary.

BONGANI: Then tell me, where is the rest of my money?

ANDILE: It must have fallen out my pocket on the way here, Bra Bongani.

BONGANI: You think I'm stupid?

ANDILE: I wouldn't steal from you. You my friend man … my boss. The cops have been hassling me, they took some of my *goof* from me last week.

BONGANI: You think I'm stupid?

ANDILE: No.

BONGANI: What am I going to tell my boss, eh, when he comes for his money? I have a family to feed. You want to see us all starve?

ANDILE: I'm serious, bra. I had it earlier.

BONGANI: You smoked it, didn't you?

ANDILE: No

BONGANI: Just tell me! [*No answer.*] Tell me!

ANDILE: Only a little bit, Bra Bongani.

BONGANI: You wasting my fucking time.

ANDILE: Please … I'll make it up to you.

BONGANI: *Uwena shlama!*

ANDILE: I only tried a little to keep the *arosta* away while I was working. You don't know what that pain is like.

BONGANI: I'm not here to fund your filthy habits. You want to be my runner then I have to be able to trust you.

ANDILE: It won't happen again.

BONGANI: That's what you said the last time.

ANDILE: It won't.

BONGANI: I'm a patient man, Andile. Four years in prison taught me this. After your aunt kicked you out her house I was the one that took you in and let you crash on my floor. I've fed you … bailed you out from the police station over and over again. I've looked after you and this is how you repay me eh? [*Beat.*]

ANDILE: I need some more *goof* to sell.

BONGANI: Not until you have paid me in full.

> BONGANI *begins to leave and* ANDILE *calls after him in desperation.*

ANDILE: I have a new client. [*Pause.*] The one you wanted. [BONGANI *stops in his tracks.*] The policewoman's son.

BONGANI [*turning back to him*]: Lieutenant Mthembu's boy?

ANDILE: Ya … ya he's in deep, Bra Bongani. [*Pause.*] You have the insurance you were looking for.

Silence.

BONGANI [*reluctantly*]: I'm giving you till Sunday
    afternoon to find my money. No more *goof* till you've
    paid off all your debt. Do you hear me?

ANDILE: Please Bra Bongani … I just need …

BONGANI [*interrupting sharply*]: You understand?

ANDILE *nods before scrambling offstage.*

Scene 13

OUTSIDE EMMANUEL'S SPHAZA SHOP

We hear a commotion off stage. EMMANUEL *enters, chasing* SIPHO *from his shop.* SIPHO *darts across the stage.*

EMMANUEL [*yelling after* SIPHO]: Sipho Mthembu, I am a friend of your mother. A friend of your family for ten years now and this is how you treat me? Stealing money from out of my till in broad daylight. [*He shakes his head sadly.*] How do I tell this to your mother? How do I tell her her only son is now smoking this rubbish?

Scene 14

OUTSIDE EMMANUEL'S SPHAZA SHOP

ANDILE *enters, followed by* SIPHO. *They are both in the grip of a* rosta, *scratching and sweating.* SIPHO *is counting the money he stole moments ago from* EMMANUEL.

SIPHO: I have it bad.

ANDILE: Me too, *mshana.*

SIPHO: Please, Andile, give me a smoke. I have some of your money. I'll find the rest later. I promise.

ANDILE: I'm dry.

SIPHO: Dry?

ANDILE: All out.

SIPHO: Nothing.

ANDILE: Nothing.

SIPHO [*freaking out*]: How am I going to get high?

ANDILE: I don't have any *goof* on me. I got into some trouble bra. I have to pay off some debt first.

SIPHO: But I need a hit now!

ANDILE: So do I … So do I.

SIPHO: How much you need to pay off your debt?

ANDILE: *Two sgodo.*

SIPHO: Two thousand!!!

ANDILE: You can help me bra.

SIPHO: How? I only have … [*He counts the money he has stolen from Emmanuel.*] R200 and that's for my smoke today.

ANDILE [*looking at* SIPHO's *neck*]: What about that?

Music begins: an ominous underscoring. SIPHO *looks down at the ring hanging around his neck, then back up at* ANDILE.

SIPHO: This?

ANDILE: Come on, Siphs.

SIPHO [*trying to change the subject*]: What about your aunty's house? Let's hit that again.

ANDILE: She kicked me out again last week. [*He is desperate.*] There isn't a doorknob or lightfitting left to steal from that house. [*Pause.*] Give me the ring.

ANDILE *tries to snatch the ring and the two fight.* ANDILE *forces* SIPHO *to the ground in a headlock …*

ANDILE: It's gold, nê? Give it to me.

SIPHO: It belonged to my father.

ANDILE: *Asina-choice,* bra!

SIPHO: It's all I have left …

ANDILE: There's no time for sentimentality Cheese boy. [*Threatening.*] *Indlala ibanga ulaka.* We need to get high.

Again ANDILE *tries to snatch the ring and* SIPHO *is forced to fight him off.*

SIPHO: I can't.

ANDILE: The pain is only going to get worse.

SIPHO: Please don't make me do this.

Music takes a darker turn. SIPHO *winces from his stomach cramps, removing the necklace and clutching it in his hand. In a repetition of the earlier rope image, the cast, their faces concealed by balaclavas, move around him winding the ropes around his stomach. As they pull from each direction the rope tightens and the pain becomes unbearable, bringing* SIPHO *to his knees.*

ANDILE: *Listen* to me. We just loan it to my boss in the meantime … 'til we can pay it off. You and I do some running … get some new kids at the school hooked and pay it off in no time. [*Pause.*] Trust me.

SIPHO *has no choice but to submit. He reluctantly holds the necklace out to* ANDILE. *The cast tugs at the ropes and* SIPHO *lets out a moan. The ring falls into* ANDILE's *open palm.* SIPHO *collapses to the floor and* ANDILE *exits.*

The light fades.

Scene 15

BONGANI'S HOUSE

ANDILE *and* SIPHO *are standing nervously before* BONGANI, *who is inspecting the ring, holding it up to the light.*

ANDILE: It's gold, nê. The real deal.

BONGANI: Why should I trust you?

ANDILE: You can't fake that shit, bra.

BONGANI *taps the ring against his teeth.*

BONGANI [*to* SIPHO]: It's real?

SIPHO: My mother gave it to me.

    BONGANI *laughs.*

BONGANI [*slipping the ring on his finger*]: The wedding ring of Lieutenant Mthembu.

SIPHO [*confused*]: You know her?

BONGANI: Everyone knows 'the good lieutenant'. [*Sarcastically.*] You could say we're old friends. [*He looks at the ring.*] What am I supposed to do with this? [*He turns to* ANDILE *and kneels.*] Are you asking for my hand in marriage?

    BONGANI *laughs loudly, the others join in nervously.*

ANDILE: We want to put it down as insurance until we can pay it off.

BONGANI [*acknowledging* SIPHO]: You know I don't like to leave guests in my house standing around. [*To* ANDILE.] Get him a chair.

ANDILE [*anxious and scratching*]: Ai, Bongani, we don't

have time for chit-chat. We need to get the *goof* and hit the street.

BONGANI [*firmly*]: I said pull up a chair!

ANDILE *gets* SIPHO *a chair and* BONGANI *gestures politely for him to sit.*

BONGANI: Sipho, is that right?

SIPHO *nods nervously.*

BONGANI: You must understand, Sipho, I have to be very careful of letting anyone of Andile's *iphara* friends work for me.

SIPHO: I'm not like his other friends, *Malume.*

BONGANI: Please, call me Bongani. [*Pause.*] What you need to understand, Sipho, is I'm just a small part of a very big business. So when you *ipharas* at the bottom start smoking the goods instead of selling it like you're supposed to … that harms me. You understand?

SIPHO: I understand.

BONGANI: That harms my business … my family … my safety. Do you follow?

SIPHO: [*nodding*]: I follow.

BONGANI: My family always comes first, you hear?

SIPHO: Yes.

BONGANI: When someone threatens my children's future it makes me very angry. [*Pause.*] So you reckon you two can sell four *sgodos* worth by the end of the weekend?

BONGANI *cuts the drug, separating it into two halves.*

SIPHO: We can, *Malume.*

BONGANI [*correcting him*]: Bongani.

41

SIPHO: I mean, Bongani.

BONGANI: I'm giving you until Sunday 5 o'clock.

ANDILE: We'll have your money by then, no worries.

BONGANI: This your final warning, Andile … Do you hear me, boy?

ANDILE: Yes Boss.

BONGANI: Your final one.

ANDILE *and* SIPHO *exit.*

Scene 16

OUTSIDE EMMANUEL'S SPHAZA SHOP

ANDILE *sits rolling a joint.* SIPHO *hovers impatiently over him, scratching himself. The bed is placed on its side and facing the audience, the springs might resemble a barbed wire fence.*

SIPHO: Hurry up, bra.

ANDILE: I'm hurrying.

SIPHO [*clutching his belly and pacing*]: When this deal is over [*Beat.*] I'm finished with this shit. I hate it, no one takes us seriously … no one cares about us. Even when you want to say something nobody listens. We are a joke, Andile … a fucking joke. I don't like what I've become. My whole life has come to a standstill. From Monday to Sunday all I can think about is smoking. [*Pause.*] I want my old life back. I want to be the person I was before.

ANDILE: Shut up, *wena*.

ANDILE *lights the whoonga joint and they each take a toke.* SIPHO *inhales deeply and leans back onto the springs of the bed, which is still standing upright and facing the audience.*

Music. TWO CAST MEMBERS *now control the bed's slow descent to the floor.* SIPHO *is lying on it as it moves from the vertical to the horizontal. The image magically suggests the intense relief and all too brief transcendence of* SIPHO'S *high. As the bed lands back on earth* ANDILE *shrinks off into the shadows.*

Scene 17

SIPHO'S ROOM

PORTIA *enters carrying a bowl of food.* SIPHO *is asleep on the bed.*

PORTIA [*concerned*]: Sipho … Sipho.

No answer from SIPHO. PORTIA *shakes him.*

PORTIA: You still haven't eaten. You must eat something.
[*Still no answer.*] I'm calling the doctor.
SIPHO: I'm fine, Ma …
PORTIA: This is your fourth day off from school.
SIPHO: It's just a tummy bug. I'm okay.
PORTIA: I've never seen you like this.
SIPHO: I'll be better in the morning.
PORTIA: Eat something.

SIPHO *mumbles pathetically.*

PORTIA: You must try.

Scene 18

EMMANUEL'S SPHAZA SHOP

PORTIA *remains watching over her son in a freeze.*
EMMANUEL *enters downstage carrying a portable radio.*
We hear the crackle of static as he tunes the radio, finally
arriving at a live Zulu broadcast of a speech by King
Goodwill Zwelithini.[5] He listens intently, fear written across
his face.

KING GOODWILL: The time is now for us to have a say. I
would like to ask the South African government to
help us. We must deal with our own lice. In our heads,
let's take out the ants and leave them in the sun. We
are asking that immigrants must take their bags and
go where they come from. It is painful for me when I
look at the country that our forefathers and thousands
of people fought for becoming a criminal den. As I'm
talking to you now, there are all sorts of things outside
the stores, they brought untidiness to our streets, it's
filthy, you can't even see what these stores were [with]
foreigners in these areas.

Yells from a crowd, offstage. Angry accusatory voices.
EMMANUEL, *fearing for his life, vanishes.*

Scene 19

CAPTAIN'S OFFICE

CAPTAIN: Lieutenant, I need you and your team on high alert this week.

PORTIA: What's going on out there?

CAPTAIN: You heard about the King's speech?

PORTIA: Yes.

CAPTAIN: There have been outbreaks of violence reported against foreign shopowners. The people are claiming the foreigners are selling whoonga to schoolchildren.

PORTIA: Not every foreigner living in this country is a dealer, for god's sake.

CAPTAIN [*shrugging*]: The people are fed up and frustrated. They're looking for someone – something – to blame. [*Grimly.*] A Somalian was set alight in his container in B-section last night.

PORTIA: Jesus.

CAPTAIN: We're anticipating more disruptions over the next few days. I'm going to need as many patrol vehicles down on the ground as possible.

PORTIA: I'll get onto it.

PORTIA *makes to leave.*

CAPTAIN: Lieutenant.

PORTIA: Yes.

CAPTAIN: Be careful.

Scene 20

BEHIND THE POLICE STATION

In what seems to be a repeat of the first scene we hear police sirens, see flashing red and blue police lights and the frantic searching of flashlights in the blackout. A boy, his face hidden by a black hoodie, comes running through the audience and onto the stage.

PORTIA [*yelling from the audience*]: You run, I shoot. Do you hear me? You hear? I will pull this trigger.

Members of the Metro Police force are hot on the criminal's heels. Again, PORTIA *leads the chase. The policemen all point their flashlights at the boy.* PORTIA, *flanked by the rest of her unit [including officers* BULAWAYO *and* ZIKHALI*] form a semi-circle around the figure.*

BULAWAYO: Down on the ground! Face down, boy.

The boy tries to dash but is pushed down to the ground by OFFICER ZIKHALI.

PORTIA: On the ground. You hear me?

The officers pin the boy to the ground with his face down.

PORTIA: Empty his pockets … empty them.

The OFFICERS *take out two packets of whoonga straws.* THE BOY *struggles, but they have him firmly in their grip.*

PORTIA: Having a busy night, nê? Planning on throwing a big party, eh? You know you could go to prison for a long time for carrying this amount of drugs. [*Beat.*] You going to tell us where you are getting all this? Even better, you're going to show us where you are getting this. Do you understand?

THE BOY *mumbles something into his hoody, his face still pressed into the ground.*

PORTIA [*to the officers*]: I can't hear him. Show me his face.

THE OFFICERS *pull* THE BOY *to his feet and hold him up. All the torch beams focus on his face.* BULAWAYO *removes his hood and reveals* SIPHO. *A moment of stunned silence and recognition.* PORTIA *clocks* SIPHO. SIPHO *clocks* PORTIA.

ZIKHALI: Let's make him eat it, Lieutenant.

BULAWAYO: Ja, Eat it!

PORTIA [*intervening*]: Wait, wait this one is a first time offender. Let him go. Let his arms go. [*She pulls the men off her son.*] Give me some time alone with him.

The POLICEMEN *reluctantly step back.*

PORTIA [*brusquely*]: Stand up. Stand up. Sipho, stand up.

SIPHO: I am sorry, Mama.

PORTIA [*dumbstruck … a long silence … softly*]: You are going to take me to the place where you got this.

SIPHO: He will kill me, Ma.

PORTIA [*softly*]: Right now. [*Angrily.*] Njengamanje!

Scene 21

BONGANI'S HOUSE

PORTIA *enters with* SIPHO, *who lingers anxiously in the background. She stands clasping Sipho's packet of whoonga straws.* BONGANI *and* PORTIA *stare at each other for a few beats.*

BONGANI: Lieutenant, how kind of you to make a house call.

PORTIA: Mr Mseleku, I think this belongs to you.

PORTIA *throws down the stock at* BONGANI's *feet.*

PORTIA: I should arrest you right now. Fast track my promotion at the police station.

BONGANI: Did you bring an extra pair of handcuffs? I think your son will be joining me.

PORTIA: Is this your idea of revenge, Mr Mseleku?

BONGANI: I like to think of it as 'insurance' for the future, Lieutenant.

PORTIA: Insurance?

BONGANI: Your son was found with five hundred grams of whoonga or brown heroin on him tonight. That's what … mmm? Ten to fifteen years in prison? [*Pause.*] Are you planning to arrest him … treat him like a filthy criminal … Drop him on the other side of the township with no money or light to find his way home. Handing him over to the station would be the right thing to do. No? Surely the law must now take its course?

49

PORTIA: You tricked him, my only child. [PORTIA *pulls her gun on* BONGANI. *He raises his hands.*] You set this trap and he fell right in, u*yinja*! You want to see him go to prison? My only child.

SIPHO: Ma, don't!

PORTIA: *Thula wena!!*

> BONGANI *stands with his hands raised but loses none of his composure.*

BONGANI [*talking down to* PORTIA *in a calm, clear voice*]: I wouldn't wish a prison sentence on anyone, Lieutenant. Do you know how hard it is to find work with a criminal record? [*Pause.*] You think I chose to be a dealer after I came out of prison? [*Pause.*] You see, my sister is an addict … she has three children … and no husband. I am the one that has to provide for all of them. When I came out of jail at the start of this year dealing whoonga was the only career option open to me.[6] [*Pause.*] I don't do this because I enjoy it. I had other far more exciting dreams for myself. You put an end to those. [*Beat.*] I do this now to survive and that is all.

> BONGANI *gestures for* PORTIA *to sit … she does.*

> *Pause.*

BONGANI: When you arrested me all those years ago you didn't even ask to hear my side of the story.

PORTIA: My job is to make arrests. The court based its decision on evidence collected at the scene of the crime.

BONGANI: The court made their decisions on rumours, not evidence. [*Pause.*] Rumours can be dangerous things, Lieutenant. Rumours cost me four years of my life in the end.

PORTIA: The Captain will hear about this. We'll close you down, send you back where you belong.

BONGANI [*laughing*]: The Captain? [*Pause.*] Who do you think is paying for his children's expensive schooling? His wife's new car? [*Beat.*]

PORTIA *sits silently.*

BONGANI: It's late. My advice to you now is to go home … take your Sipho with you. From now on you protect me and my business and I'll make sure that no one finds out about your son's activities. *Izandla ziyagezana.*

PORTIA [*standing up*]: Are you blackmailing me?

BONGANI: I prefer to see it as coming to some sort of agreement.

BONGANI *pulls the wedding ring out and hands it to* PORTIA.

PORTIA: You are ruining my life.

A brief pause.

BONGANI: You reap what you sow … *Uvuna okutshalile.*

Lights fade.

Scene 22

PORTIA'S HOUSE

The bed is placed centre stage and SIPHO *lies down on it.*
PORTIA *turns to address the audience. Repetitive music plays*
under the next sequence, suggesting a sort of delirium.

PORTIA: I should have seen the signs. I was so busy
    pursuing the problem in the back alleys of KwaMashu
    that I didn't notice it creep into my own home. How
    could I have been so blind? And now where to? What
    must a mother do? They say there is no end to this
    nightmare … that once a child is addicted you might
    as well consider them dead … But I won't surrender,
    Sipho. [PORTIA *removes the handcuffs from her belt.*]
    I won't leave your side until we have driven these
    demons away. All I have is patience and love … that's
    all I can give.

   PORTIA *gently takes* SIPHO's *left hand and handcuffs it*
   to the bedpost.

SIPHO [*clutching his belly with his right hand*]: It's painful,
    Ma … It's sore.
PORTIA: I know my boy … I know.
SIPHO: Let me free, Ma. [*He rattles the handcuffs against the*
    metal frame.]
PORTIA: I can't.
SIPHO [*yelling*]: Let me go!
PORTIA: Not until the poison has left your system.

SIPHO: Let me go!

PORTIA: It's only been two days. Eat some porridge … here.

> PORTIA *holds out a bowl of porridge.*

SIPHO [*crying*]: Let me go, Ma!

PORTIA: Those people in the community will kill you if they catch you stealing from them again. This is for your own safety my boy. [*Pause.*] Try and eat.

> SIPHO *strikes the bowl from out of her hands and the contents scatter across the stage. He writhes in pain.* PORTIA *goes on her hands and knees to clean up the spilt porridge.*

> SIPHO, *still delirious with arosta, tosses and turns.* ANDILE *enters and hovers over the bed … a hallucination perhaps? Only* SIPHO *appears to sense his presence and calls out.*

SIPHO: Andile … Andile …

PORTIA: Andile isn't here.

SIPHO: Get me Andile.

> SIPHO *grasps at the air frantically with his free hand.*

PORTIA [*adamantly*]: That *isigebengu* won't put a foot in this house.

SIPHO: I need Andile.

PORTIA: You will never smoke that rubbish again!

> ANDILE *vanishes back into the shadows of Sipho's room.*

SIPHO: I need to smoke, Mamma. The pain is killing me. [*He yells.*] Andile! Andile!

PORTIA: I can't let you do that.

SIPHO: I'm dying …

PORTIA: So that you can live again soon. It's been four days, Sipho … Why go back?

SIPHO *collapses again.*

PORTIA [*turning back to the audience*]: You must understand. [*She is exhausted.*] I tried everything I could. Not even God could heal him.

OFF-STAGE VOICES *praying.* THREE MEN *from the church enter, laying their hands on* SIPHO *in the bed and praying wildly.*

VOICE 1: Yea, though I walk through the valley of the shadow of death, I will fear no evil, for thou art with me; thy rod and thy staff they comfort me …

VOICE 2: May this demon be cast out of this poor boy …

VOICE 3: May the blood of Christ wash over him and cleanse his blood of this poison …

VOICE 4: Behold the Cross of The Lord, flee bands of enemies …

PORTIA [*praying quietly, desperately*]: Will this ever stop? Will I ever sleep? Will I wake from this nightmare? Sweet Jesus, bring me peace!

PORTIA and all the voices together: Amen.

PORTIA *tries to lift* SIPHO's *head and get him to drink water. He drinks thirstily, the water spilling over him.*

SIPHO: Ma, please let me go … Please take these off … Please Ma … Ma!

PORTIA [*to the audience*]: One of my neighbours said her son had healed himself by consulting a traditional healer, so I took him to a *sangoma* after that.

A pool of light reveals the sangoma, huddled over a mat, divining from bones and umuthi.

SANGOMA: He will need to drink this and you will need to wash his body with *uBhokodwayo* twice a day. This will help him forget. He will never turn his back on this … He will always be looking over his shoulder. His ancestors are calling him out of the city, he is drowning in this city. He must leave this city.

PORTIA [*whispering to herself*]: Will this ever stop? Will I ever sleep? Will I wake from this nightmare? Sweet Jesus bring me peace. [*To the audience.*] The social worker tried his best to guide us …

SOCIAL WORKER *enters at the side of the bed, looking down at a clipboard before addressing* PORTIA.

SOCIAL WORKER: I'm afraid, *Lieutenant* Mthembu, you will have to put his name on a list.

PORTIA: How long will we have to wait?

SOCIAL WORKER: Anywhere from one to three months.

PORTIA: We cannot wait that long, my son may be dead by then.

SOCIAL WORKER: There are only two public rehabilitation centres in this province. They fill up quickly.

PORTIA: And when he does finally go to the rehab what are the chances of him being healed?

SOCIAL WORKER: There is currently a two per cent chance of recovery.

PORTIA [*shocked*]: Two per cent? Oh God …

SOCIAL WORKER: In the meantime I suggest you try to get him into a Narcotics Anonymous group where he can speak with others. There's also a number for a private doctors who can prescribe Methadone.

PORTIA: Methadone?

SOCIAL WORKER: You know how a diabetic must take insulin to treat his diabetes? Well, Methadone, you could say, is like the insulin for heroin users … Just a word of warning though, Mrs Mthembu … [*Pause.*] *Ungaliyisa ihhashi emfuleni, kodwa ngeke uliphoqe ukuthi liphuze.*

SOCIAL WORKER *exits.* PORTIA *walks to the bed with a suitcase and bus ticket in her hands.*

PORTIA [*to audience*]: I kept him like this for two weeks. Two weeks! Until neither of us could bear it any longer.

THE CAST *begins to sing a plaintive Zulu hymn.* PORTIA *unlocks the handcuffs.* SIPHO *slowly sits up in bed, rubbing his wrists.*

SIPHO: Ma?

PORTIA *kneels beside the bed.*

PORTIA: I don't know what else I can do. I will never give up on you. I just … I just don't know what more I can do?

SIPHO *rises, and embraces her.* PORTIA *hands him the bus ticket and packed suitcase.*

PORTIA: You have to help me, Sipho. The choice needs to be yours. I cannot make it for you.

Song continues as SIPHO *leaves the scene.*

Scene 23

CAPTAIN'S OFFICE

Shouts and sirens from off stage. The CAPTAIN *and* PORTIA *enter.*

CAPTAIN: Lieutenant, we need you and your team on the ground.

PORTIA: We are on our way, Captain.

CAPTAIN: Mobs of people are moving through the township burning sphaza shops and calling for the heads of dealers. This morning they killed a young man from the township. They beat him to death after they found him carrying whoonga.

PORTIA: I'm on my way, Captain.

Sound of angry mob increases. PORTIA *exits.*

Scene 24

EMMANUEL'S SPHAZA SHOP

EMMANUEL's *store is burning. A MOB OF ANGRY MEN armed with pangas and knobkerries throws him onto the stage.*

ATTACKER 1: We have him. We have the dealer!

ATTACKER 2: Get out of here *Kwerekwere*!

ATTACKER 1: Burn him!

EMMANUEL: Please … Please … don't …

ATTACKER 3: He's ruining our children's lives.

ATTACKER 2: He must pay. This one must pay now!

EMMANUEL: I've done nothing wrong.

Blue and red siren lights flash on the stage. We hear shots being fired. PORTIA *arrives on the scene forcing the mob away from* EMMANUEL.

PORTIA: People! People! This man is not a dealer! This is not justice!

ATTACKER 1 [*shouting*]: Burn him!

ATTACKER 2: Burn the *kwerekwere*!

PORTIA [*addressing the crowd and the audience*]: You blame this man for all our problems? How easy it is to blame one man for so many things. So easy to wash your hands clean with another's life. You are quick to judge users and accuse Emmanuel today, but it doesn't seem to bother you, that *you* are the ones giving our children the money for whoonga. [*Beat.*] *Iqaqa alizizwa ukunuka,* none of us is innocent!

CROWD MEMBER [*shouting*]: But he is a dealer, he must go!

PORTIA: You don't know that. [*Beat.*] Actually, *you* know who the real dealers are in D Section. I know there are dealers in this community who pay your children's school fees to buy your loyalty … [*Pause.*] You can go ahead and blame Emmanuel … you can blame our kids for stealing … you can blame the police for not doing enough, but what do we do with all this blame? We can't eat blame, we can't smoke it, we can't sell it … We just move it around, like we do with the users. We just move them around from one area to the next, because we don't want to deal with the real issues here. What happens to one of us happens to all of us!

PORTIA *helps* EMMANUEL *to his feet.*

PORTIA: This problem isn't someone else's. It's all of ours … It's all of ours.

Music rises. THE CROWDS *disperse.*

Scene 25

ON THE STREET

SIPHO *enters with his suitcase, calling out Andile's name. There is no answer*

SIPHO: Andile … Andile!

> SIPHO *sees* ANDILE's *body crumpled in a heap on the floor and rushes over to it.* PORTIA *enters upstage and watches.*

SIPHO: Andile … Andile! [*He shakes the body and it does not move.*] Andile!

> PORTIA *places a hand on her son's shoulder and shakes her head sadly. Lights fade on the tableau.*

Epilogue

OUR STORY

A circle of chairs on the stage as in the first scene. PORTIA *is at the cente and* SIPHO *sits beside her. The rest of* THE CAST *occupy the chairs.*

PORTIA: This is where I'll end my story tonight. After listening to all the stories here I guess we might be considered the lucky ones. So many communities torn apart. So many young lives lost … but we are both still here. [*Pause.*] When Sipho returned from his gogo we went to visit the doctor that the social worker had suggested to us. He is now on Methadone treatment … We have to pay for it but it's helping. [*Pause.*] We are taking it day by day now, we try to be more patient, more gentle with each other. We share our stories and we listen, and by listening … we begin to heal.

Lights fade. The acappella hymn 'Somebody', by the King's Messengers Quartet begins.

THE END

Notes

1. Sadly, the person who inspired the story of Bongani
    was killed in 2016 in what seems to have been a violent
    drug-related altercation.

2. We named this character after Emmanuel Sithole, who
    was brutally murdered during the 2015 xenophobic
    attacks in Durban, while we were creating this script
    and conducting research. We named the character after
    him and have dedicated the play to him.

3. The current punitive models for drug possession
    and consumption in South Africa are monitored by
    arrest quotas, which were established by the South
    African Police Service. For this reason many officers
    feel they are under enormous pressure to make more
    arrests each month. They also feel they must appease
    the media and suburban residents who blamed
    the majority of the crime in their communities on
    whoonga consumers and dealers. The pathologising
    of whoonga users by the media further fuelled these
    pressures, which, in turn, made holistic, collaborative,
    harm-reduction processes less possible as the police
    felt they had to 'clean up' the whoonga problem using
    primarily punitive processes.

4. *Arosta* is the name for the pains that occur as a side
    effect of smoking whoonga. They include itching, pain
    in the stomach, joint pain, headaches and sneezing.
    The pains are caused by the use of Rattex, a rat poison
    containing strychnine, which is mixed into the heroin

to prevent the user's blood from clotting. Strychnine helps keep the blood flowing, preventing embolisms and ensuring the user lives to purchase the next hit. As the body builds immunity to the substance, the blood begins to form small clots in the veins, which often causes whoonga users to scratch compulsively. The average whoonga user in Durban spends about R100 to R150 a day to keep the arosta at bay.

5. While we were conducting our research, King Goodwill Zwelithini delivered a speech in Pongola, which allegedly fuelled the xenophobic attacks that broke out in the city a few weeks later. We found ourselves rehearsing in the midst of brutal xenophobic violence, right outside the rehearsal spaces at the Denis Hurely Centre in the CBD. Each day, the Big Brotherhood team witnessed foreign nationals fleeing their homes in KwaMashu to stay in refugee camps in the city. A recurring theme of blame emerged among various people we interviewed: they held the foreign nationals responsible for the whoonga epidemic in their communities – yet there was no evidence to support this. Of the entire foreign national community in Durban only a fraction has been found to be involved in the dealing of drugs.

6. Our research revealed that first time ex-convicts are offered around R10 000 as a 'starter pack' by a local network of dealers who are also ex-convicts, to set up their own franchise. The dealers we interviewed said

they could pay this off within a month and have a fully-fledged business within two weeks. It's recognised that arresting drug users is possibly one of the worst ways of responding to the issue. Not only is our prison system overflowing, throwing into prison people who are drug users themselves, or from areas riddled with gangsterism, creates more work and more potential problems down the road.

The authors

The Big Brotherhood is an award-winning theatre and production company based in Durban. Formed by a dynamic group of artists – Vumani Khumalo, Phumlani Ngubane, Ngcebo Cele, Sandile Nxumalo and Zenzo Msomi, it started under the wing of KwaMashu Community Advancement Projects, creating productions about crime and jail life and performing them in schools and theatres in KwaZulu-Natal. Managed by the artists themselves, it was one of the first groups affiliated to the Twist Theatre Development Project. More than a theatre company, it is also a social development learning laboratory that aims to create socially relevant theatre in South Africa, honouring the memory of the powerful struggle theatre-makers of the past.

Empatheatre, co-founded by Dylan McGarry, Neil Coppen and Mpume Mthombeni, is a theatre company that uses an emerging trans-disciplinary theatre methodology to bring together various forums – documentary, verbatim, research and applied theatre models. Inspired by South African struggle theatre, the theatre of the oppressed, Empatheatre researches and shares people's real-life stories, with the intention of inspiring and developing a greater empathy and kindness in complex social learning spaces beset by conflict or injustice. Empatheatre forms part of the wider Transgressive Learning Research School and the Transformations Knowledge Network, within the International Social Science Council.

Mpume Mthombeni is an award-winning performer and theatre-maker who hails from Umlazi, Durban. She has played multiple roles over the years in theatre, radio, film and television, attracting international acclaim for her performance in *Tin Bucket Drum*, which she took to New York in 2012. Other theatre credits include *Animal Farm*, *Soil & Ash*, *NewFoundLand* and *Ulwembu*. Her work with Empatheatre focuses on merging research and performance and she considers the theatre-maker's role in contemporary South Africa to be that of healer and shaman.

Neil Coppen is an award-winning writer, director, designer and multimedia artist living in Durban. Among his awards was the 2011 Standard Bank Young Artist Award for Drama and he is one of six South African playwrights to have been granted a staged reading of his work at The Royal Court Theatre in London. Some of Neil's most acclaimed works are *Tin Bucket Drum*, *Tree Boy*, *Abnormal Loads* and *Izipopolo*. His local, all-female cast adaptation of George Orwell's *Animal Farm* toured the country for more than five years, playing to capacity houses in Johannesburg, Durban and Cape Town. Coppen's latest play, *NewFoundLand/Buite Land* premiered at the 2017 Klein Karoo Nasionale Kunstefees and won the Kana Award for Best Debut Production.

Dylan McGarry, an environmental anthropologist, educational sociologist and artist based in Durban, is a post-doctoral researcher at the Environmental Learning

Research Centre at Rhodes University and a research fellow for the Transgressive Learning Research School. He has a transdisciplinary PhD in Environmental Education and Art (social sculpture). His work to date has mainly revolved around sustainable rural development, informal youth education in complex learning environments and social ecological learning in various contexts and cultures.

Printed and bound by CPI Group (UK) Ltd, Croydon, CR0 4YY

13/04/2025

14656584-0001